LOOK & FIND EASTER HUNT

CLEVER Publishing

T0004423

Find the Easter Bunny
who is playing guitar.
How many
Easter Bunnies
are wearing hats?
Which Easter Bunny
has a paintbrush?

23
Find all the Easter Bunnies carrying baskets.
Which Easter Bunny is nibbling on a carrot?
Which two Easter Bunnies are identical?

Which egg is decorated
like a bunny?
Find all the eggs
with polka dots.
Count all the pink-and-yellow
striped eggs.

Find the egg with
a star on it.
Uh-oh! How many cracked
eggs do you see?
Find all the
eggs with
smiley faces.

Look for the basket that's filled with only eggs.
How many chocolate bunnies do you see?
Find the basket with a bunny in it.

How many baskets have a bow on them?
Count all the strawberries.
Find two identical baskets.

How many cats do you see?
Point to all the bunnies.
Which puppy wears a bow?

Count all the fluffy sheep.
Find two identical llamas.
Count all the yellow chicks.

How many lollipops do you count?
Point to all the marshmallow chicks.
Which chocolate bunnies have been bitten already?
CH

How many gummy worms can you find?
Point to all the cupcakes with sprinkles.
Find all the peppermints.

How many carrots do you count?
Find all of the chocolate muffins.
Find the pie with cherries on top.

Find the strawberry jam jars.
Point to your favorite food on the page.
Count all the bananas.

This is a dandelion. How many more can you find?

Which bouquet has three pink flowers in it?

Find all the purple flowers.

How many kids have flowers in their hair?

Point to the tallest flower on the page.

Find two flowers identical to this one.

How many rainbows are there?
Find all the umbrellas with polka dots on them.
Count all of the butterflies.

Point to the smallest bumblebee.
How many rain clouds do you see?
Find the matching pair of rain boots.

How many snails can you count?
Find all the shovels with yellow handles.
Which flowerpots have stripes on them?

Point to all the watering cans.
Count all the red tomatoes.
Where are the yellow gardening gloves?

How many picnic blankets do you count?

Find two chocolate bunnies.

Point to all the bicycles.

Find all the hidden Easter eggs.

Point to the picnic basket with a blue bow around it.

Which two swans are identical?

EASTER GAME

You will need chips or coins (one per player) and a die. Place the chips or coins on START. Each player rolls the die and moves forward the number spaces shown on the die. If a player lands on an Easter egg, they must hop like a bunny. If a player lands on a flower, they must sing a song. If a player lands on a leaf, they must make sounds like a bird. The first player to reach the basket wins!

START

COLLECT THE SERIES:

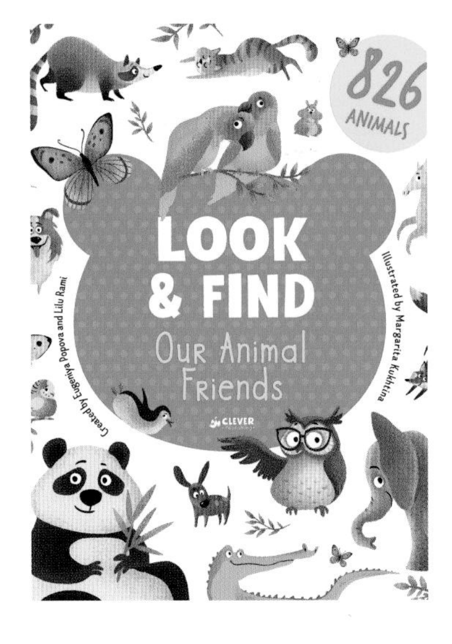

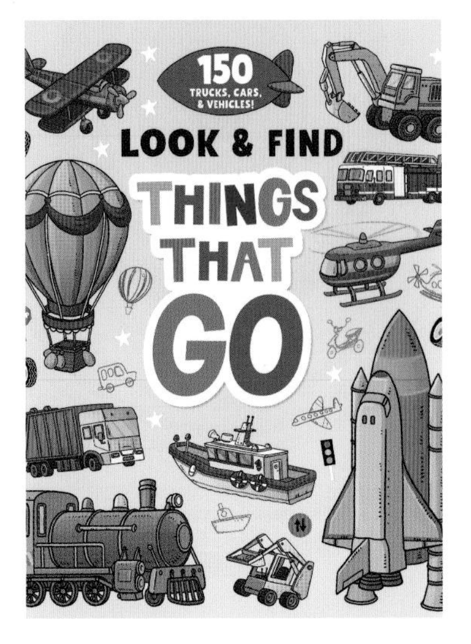

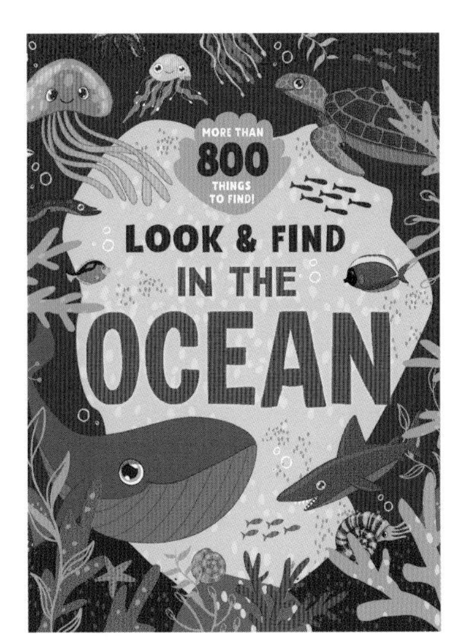

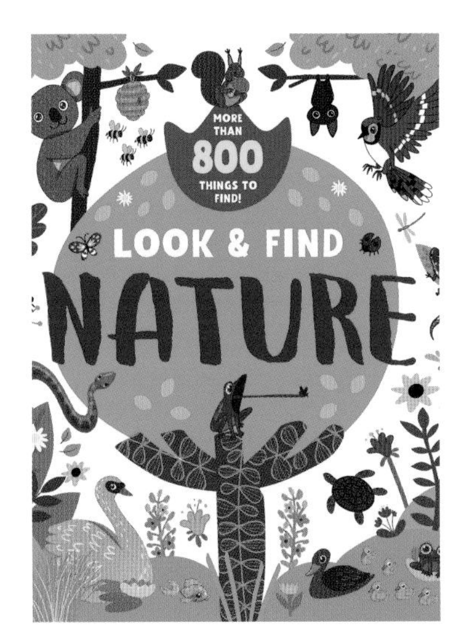

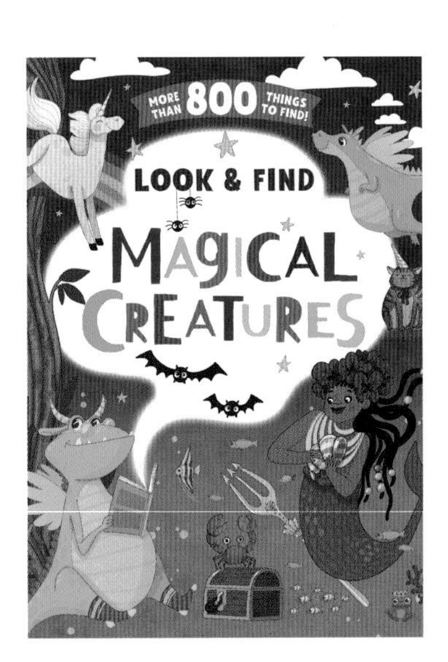